Live • Work • Play • Learn

GALLOPADE INTERNATIONAL

Gallopade International is introducing SAT words that kids need to know in our books. The SAT words in this book have a gray box around them. Students can look up the definitions and increase their vocabulary. Happy Learning!

Gallopade is proud to be a member and supporter of these educational organizations and associations:

Association for the Study of African American Life and History
National Alliance of Black School Educators
American Booksellers Association
American Library Association
International Reading Association
National Association for Gifted Children
The National School Supply and Equipment Association
The National Council for the Social Studies
Museum Store Association
Association of Partners for Public Lands
Association of Booksellers for Children

At the time of publication, all websites referenced in this document were valid. However, due to the changing nature of the Internet, some addresses may change or the content become less relevant.

It's Your World Books

Africa: A Safari Through Its Amazing Nations!

Australia: The Land Down Under for Mates of All Ages!

Canada: The Maple Leaf Melting Pot Country!

China: A Great Wall Runs Thru It!

Egypt: An Ancient Land of Lore; a Modern Land of Oil and More!

France: The Ooh-La-La Country Everyone Loves!

Germany: The Country of Fairytale Castles and Cutting Edge Science!

Greece: A Volcanic Land of Ancient Olympic Origins!

India: Land of Six Senses and Intriguing Mystery!

Italy: The Country of Amazing Fountains and Awesome Arts!

Japan: An Island Country of Endless Intrigue!

Mexico: A Colorful Land of Exotic Culture!

Middle East: Ancient Countries of Current Events Headlines!

Russia: The Great Bear and Its Dramatic History!

South America: A Continent of Countries of Amazing Proportions!

United Kingdom: The Country of Ships, Sealing Wax, Cabbages, and Kings!

Other Carole Marsh Related Titles:
**The Mystery at the Roman Colosseum
Italian for Kids**

Table of Contents

A Letter from the Author

From the desk of
CAROLE MARSH

Hey kids,

It's your world! It really, really is!
Of course, you already know that, don't you?
You surf the 'net, listen to satellite radio, watch television shows and movies set all around the globe—kids today are much more "worldly" than in the past and that's a good thing!

Now's a great time to learn something about another country—such as Italy. Why? Because one day, you might actually visit there (if you have not already!). You might go to school there—many colleges have ties with international schools around the globe. You might even go on to work in a foreign country!

Many companies have positions in other countries. Companies are "going global" as fast as they can. They have branch offices, manufacturing plants, and customer service centers scattered around the globe!

So, ready or not: YOU are a Citizen of the World! And you'll want to be a good one.
How do you do that? You'll find out everything you can about that country, how it's the same, and how it's different from your own country. What language is spoken there? What customs do the people observe? What foods do they enjoy? What do they do for fun? What has happened in this part of the world, and what is happening there now? It's fun ... and the more you learn, the more you will enjoy whatever global opportunity comes your way!

This book is a good place to start your learning journey—so take advantage of the world— IT'S YOUR WORLD, after all ... and guess what? It's a BIG world, after all!

Happy traveling and learning,

Carole Marsh
Always with passport in hand!

Why Should We Care About Italy?

Italy is one of the most important countries in the world! This beautiful country is extremely popular with tourists from around the globe. Everyone wants to come and see its ancient ruins, its majestic cathedrals, the leaning tower of Pisa, the Tuscan countryside, and so much more!

Italy is a vibrant nation, active in world affairs. It is "Fashion Central" for fine clothing. It has some of the most amazing art museums and artwork in the world. And Italian food is among the best cuisine anywhere!

One day, you might visit Italy to see an opera at the famous La Scala opera house, appreciate the art collection of the Vatican, travel by train through wine country, sail on the Italian Riviera, or work for an Italian company. It could happen!

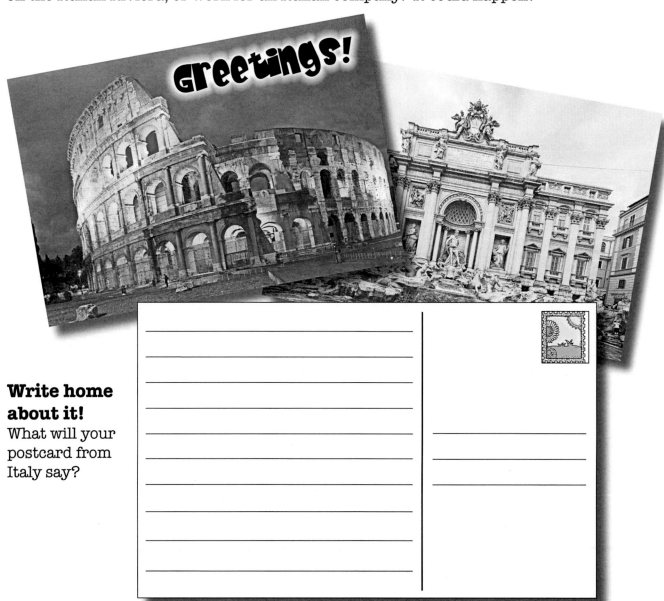

Write home about it!
What will your postcard from Italy say?

Top Fast Italy Facts!

Important facts to remember about the country of Italy:

- Italy is officially called *Repubblica Italiana*, the Republic of Italy.
- Italy has a President and a Prime Minister.
- Italy has a republican government.
- Italy is one of the major developed countries in the world. It is an ally of the United States and other nations.
- Italy is a member of the United Nations and the European Union.
- Italy has a mild Mediterranean climate.
- Italy is the fourth most-visited country in the world!
- Italy's motto is "Italy is a democratic republic, founded on labor."
- The capital of Italy is Rome.
- The official language is Italian.
- The currency used is the euro.
- About 90 percent of Italians are Roman Catholic.

Now, you figure out the rest!

1. This is the Italian ___ ___ ___ ___.

2. This is the national ___ ___ ___ ___ ___ ___ of Italy.

3. "Italy is a democratic republic, founded on labor" is the national ___ ___ ___ ___ ___.

4. The ___ ___ ___ ___ ___ ___ ___ ___ name of Italy is *Repubblica Italiana*.

5. The ___ ___ ___ ___ ___ ___ ___ ___ ___ ___ of Italy is about 57 million people.

6. The name ___ ___ ___ ___ ___ comes from a group of people in the Bronze Age called "the Itali."

Where in the World Is Italy?

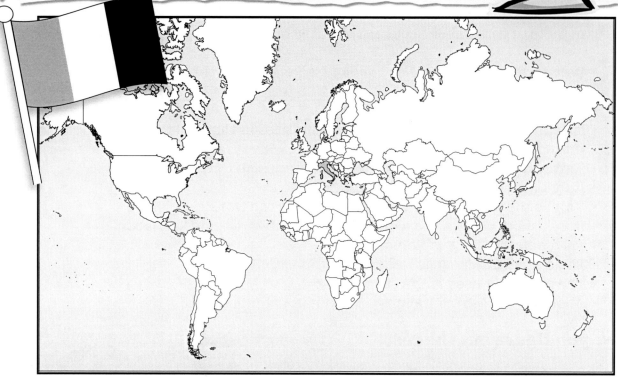

- Italy's capital city is Rome.
- Italy is a country in Europe and is sometimes known as the "boot" country.
- Italy is surrounded by the Mediterranean, Ionian, and Adriatic Seas.
- Italy's neighbors are Monaco, France, Switzerland, Austria, and Slovenia.
- Italians live in important cities like Turin, Genoa, Florence, and Naples.
- Vatican City is a tiny nation within Rome; it is the headquarters of the Roman Catholic Church.
- Italy has two major islands—Sicily and Sardinia.
- The principal mountain ranges of Italy are the Alps and the Apennines.
- The Tiber River is one of the longest rivers in Italy; it flows through Rome.
- The Italian Lakes region, nestled in the Italian Alps, is a popular tourist destination.
- Get ready for a delicious meal of spaghetti and other types of pasta!

Do You Know?

1. This river runs through Rome:
   A. Seine   B. Tiber   C. Thames

2. Italy is shaped like a:
   A. boot   B. cowboy hat   C. mitten

Ancient Rome

Who founded Rome? Legend has it that twin brothers, Romulus and Remus, established a village in 753 B.C.E. on the Palatine Hill overlooking the Tiber River. Greek legend says the Trojan hero Aeneas founded a settlement in central Italy following the Trojan War. Some legends combine the two myths, making Romulus and Remus the descendants of Aeneas.

The Roman Empire was so vast and lasted so long that its influence has been felt worldwide. Its influence can be heard in languages spoken today. Many European and Latin American nations are based on Roman law. The U.S. government is based on the ancient Roman political system. Roman structures such as roads, bridges, and aqueducts were models for engineers throughout the world. Some of the ancient Roman structures are still in use today!

Crosswords!
Use your new knowledge to fill in the crossword puzzle.

Across

4. The U.S. government is based on the ancient Roman _____ system.
6. The founding of Rome is based on _____.

Down

1. Many Western _____ are based on Roman law.
2. The Roman _____ lasted a long time.
3. Twin brothers who founded Rome, _____ and Remus.
5. Some say that Romulus and Remus are the descendants of _____ .

The Amazing History of Italy!

Italy has a long and dramatic history! Ancient Italy is best known as the Roman Empire. Julius Caesar ruled! In the 4th century, the empire was split into eastern and western halves. While the Eastern Roman Empire prospered for another 1,000 years, the Western Roman Empire (which includes today's Italy) collapsed very quickly.

From the 5th century until the 11th century, Italy was invaded, fought over, and ruled by outside powers. It became a battleground between popes and emperors. Even with these struggles, Italy grew and prospered. Great advances were made in art and in man's understanding of the world. The best-known achievement was the Italian Renaissance—a "new birth" of art and learning.

Benito Mussolini

From the 16th century until the late 1800s, Italy was defeated and conquered by foreign powers. In 1922, dictator Benito Mussolini came to power and ruled with an iron fist. Italy joined Germany and Japan as an Axis power during World War II. After the Axis powers were defeated in 1945, a new republic was born—the Republic of Italy!

Like many developed countries today, Italy struggles with economic issues, the war on terrorism, immigration, health care, climate change, and other modern problems. In the meantime, it remains a beautiful country with hopes for a great future!

Timeline!
Number these events in the order that they took place, first to last.

____ Italy fights in World War II.

____ Julius Caesar comes to power.

____ Italy enjoys commercial prosperity.

____ Benito Mussolini comes to power.

____ The Roman Empire is split in half.

____ The Renaissance begins.

____ Italy becomes unified.

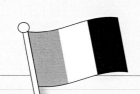

Famous Italian Folks!

Matching!

Match these famous Italian folks with their accomplishments.

_____ 1. I was a sculptor, painter, and architect who was a major influence of the Italian Baroque period. I had an impressive list of patrons, including the powerful Borghese family. My most famous work is the sculpture *Fountain of the Four Rivers* at the Piazza Navona in Rome.

_____ 2. I was a mathematician and an astronomer. I invented the microscope and built a telescope to study the heavens. One of my most important discoveries was finding the moons of Jupiter. I supported the theory that the Earth orbits the sun.

_____ 3. I was a general in the ancient Roman army. I entered Rome with my forces and took control of the Roman Empire. I declared myself dictator for life, but was murdered by members of the Senate in 44 B.C.E.

_____ 4. I was the first person to write in Italian, rather than the traditional Latin. While living in exile, I wrote my masterpiece called *The Divine Comedy*. In it, I explore heaven, hell, and purgatory with the poet Virgil as my guide.

_____ 5. As a child, I went to a performance of *Aida*, an opera by the great Giuseppe Verdi. After hearing his masterpiece, I knew that I wanted to compose operas. Many consider me to be Verdi's successor. My most famous works are *La Bohème*, *Madame Butterfly*, and *Turandot*.

_____ 6. In 1492, I set sail to find a shorter route to India. I left with three ships called the *Nina*, the *Pinta*, and the *Santa Maria*. I never made it to India. Instead, I discovered a whole new world.

A. Julius Caesar

B. Gianlorenzo Bernini

C. Dante Alighieri

D. Christopher Columbus

E. Galileo Galilei

F. Giacomo Puccini

Guts and Glory Italian Style!

A. It killed about 25 million people in Europe in the 1300s. That's about one out of every three people! It caused a fever, black spots on the chest, and big, black lumps under the arms, on the neck, and at the top of the legs. Most people who got it died screaming in pain within a few days. It was finally discovered that fleas from rats were to blame. People still get it even today, but now there is medicine to cure it.

B. This square is located in the middle of Rome. It is one of the most famous and, some believe, the most beautiful. Its shape is oval, not square. The main attractions are the three fountains—the Fountain of the Four Rivers, Neptune Fountain, and Moor Fountain.

C. The time was 44 B.C.E. Julius Caesar had just been elected dictator for life. While some were happy about this, many were not. Plots of assassination were discussed secretly and a date was set. A fortune teller approached the new emperor and warned him. But Caesar ignored him and was murdered in the Senate on this date. Shakespeare wrote that the fortune teller said, "Beware the..." What phrase did he use?

D. This group was persecuted for their beliefs in Ancient Rome. Worshipping anyone other than the emperor was cause for punishment. Many were tortured before they died. One common practice of torture was to do this as a form of entertainment for the Roman people. What was it?

E. He was a politician from Florence in the early 16th century. When the powerful Medici family came to power, he was forced to resign. He tried many times to regain his position, but he failed. He wrote *The Prince* to regain favor but the effort backfired. His book promoted success at any means, even at the expense of traditional values. His book earned the reputation for ruthlessness, deception, and cruelty. Today, his last name means "corrupt government."

Mixed Up!
Match the paragraph to the word that the paragraph describes.

FEEDING CHRISTIANS TO THE LIONS

_____

IDES OF MARCH

_____

BLACK PLAGUE

_____

NICCOLO MACHIAVELLI

_____

PIAZZA NOVONA

_____

If It Ain't "Baroque," Don't Fix It!

Fancy! Decorated! Extravagant! These are just a few words that describe the Baroque art movement. It originated in Italy in the late 1500s and lasted for about 200 years. The word "baroque" is a Portuguese word meaning "irregularly shaped pearl." Baroque artists wanted paintings to be more realistic and emotional. Sculptors and architects also created emotion, movement, and variety in their pieces.

The characteristics of baroque art are a sense of movement, energy, and tension. Even baroque buildings seem to be in motion! Artists of the time were also concerned with how the mind worked. They tried to show what someone was feeling and thinking. Realism was important, too. Check out a painting of the time. It almost looks like if you touched it, you would feel skin or cloth rather than canvas!

Many rulers and other important people encouraged this art style. They hired artists to create important works that would show off how wealthy and powerful they were. Some famous Italian Baroque artists were Paolo Veronese, Caravaggio, Gianlorenzo Bernini, and Annibale Caracci.

Draw It!
Get out your crayons. Choose someone to draw. How realistic can you make it? Would you have made a great Baroque artist?

Michelangelo, Master Artist!

Michelangelo

Painter or sculptor? You decide! Michelangelo Buonaratti is best known for his painting in the Sistine Chapel, but he always considered himself a sculptor. Michelangelo, as he is known, was born in a small village outside of Florence in 1475. He began studying painting and sculpture when he was just 13 years old.

Many agree that his most beautiful piece is the sculpture of the Pietà in St. Peter's cathedral. His other great masterpiece is the magnificent lifelike sculpture of David.

David

Portrait of Adam from the Sistine Chapel

Pope Julius II asked Michelangelo to paint the ceiling of the Sistine Chapel. He began working on the ceiling in 1508. For four years, Michelangelo stood with his neck craned backward and painted the ceiling! When it was completed, it was recognized as a masterpiece. At the age of just 37, Michelangelo was recognized as the greatest living artist!

Michelangelo produced many more great works in his life. He continued to work until his death in 1564 at the age of 89. Today, we can still see his works and recognize that he was truly a master and one of a kind!

Write home about it!

Use the letters of Michelangelo's name to create as many words with three letters or more as you can.

MICHELANGELO

_____   _____

_____   _____

_____   _____   _____

_____   _____   _____

_____   _____   _____

_____   _____   _____

_____   _____   _____

The Leaning Tower of Pisa, a Site to See!

Have you ever seen a leaning building? There's one in Italy! **The Leaning Tower of Pisa** is the *campanile*, or freestanding bell tower, of the cathedral of the Italian city of Pisa. The tower began leaning to the southeast soon after the workers started to build it in 1173. It was built on soil that could not support it. The tower presently leans to the southwest. Its construction continued, with two long interruptions, for about 200 years.

The Leaning Tower of Pisa weighs about 14,700 metric tons.

During World War II, the Allies discovered that the Nazis were using the tower as an observation post.

There are seven bells in the tower, tuned to musical scale.

The official name of the Tower of Pisa is TORRE PENDENTE DI PISA.

On January 7, 1990, after more than two decades of work on the tower, it was closed to the public.

Create your very own travel pamphlet.
Concentrate on an area that interests you. Perhaps you enjoyed learning about the people. Or maybe it was the monuments that interested you. Fold a piece of paper into three sections. This will give you six areas on which to put information.

My Favorite Place to Visit!

Last Names First!

Customs and culture vary widely from country to country. Sometimes they vary in different regions of the same country. Here are customs and cultural differences observed by Italians!

- The handshake is a common greeting between acquaintances.
- Good friends greet each other with air kisses, first near the left cheek, then near the right. Men may add a pat on the back.
- It is considered rude to use someone's first name before you are invited to do so.
- Yellow flowers are a sign of jealousy and should not be given as a gift.
- The fork is held in the left hand and the knife in the right. You hold them the opposite way!
- Italians are extremely fashion conscious, and they expect others to dress stylishly, too.
- In the summer, many people in Italy take the entire month of August off from school or work to vacation.
- Children are named for Catholic saints, and they celebrate their saint's day as if it were their own birthday!

Create your own!
Customs and cultural activities can help define who we are. Think about your family and friends, and come up with some new customs for everyone to try.

The color purple is a symbol of bad luck.

Lei parla italiano?

The official language in Italy is Italian. Italian is one of the romance languages. Italian nouns are considered either feminine (la) or masculine (il or lo).

Match it up!

Below are some common Italian phrases or words. See if you can match them to the English word.

blu   cat

rosso   red

il gatto   sister

l'oliva   thank you

il pepe   blue

sorella   olive

il cane   bicycle

il bicicletta   pepper

ciao   hello

grazie   dog

Are you talking to me?

Happy Holidays!

festival of
SPAGHETTI!

Italy enjoys many holidays and festivals. Some important holidays are **New Year's Day, Liberation Day,** and **Labor Day**. Religious holidays are also important and include **Christmas**, the *Befana*, and **Easter**.

Carnevale is a big festival held every year before Lent. One of the largest carnevales is held in Venice. The celebration lasts for nearly two weeks. People wear masks and colorful costumes. Gondolas and boats parade down the Grand Canal. On the last day of the celebration, a great fireworks show ends the festivities.

Italians also have festivals to celebrate their good food. Celebrations are held at the end of the grape-growing season. If you like spaghetti, you can visit the town of Torre Annunziata where the **Festival of Spaghetti** is held!

Write it down!
Pretend you are visiting Italy. Write a letter to your best friend. Tell him or her about Carnevale. Be sure to describe the costumes and fireworks show.

PRESENT

Italy on the Stage and in the Museums!

Italian culture has a rich history. Italy is the birthplace of Leonardo da Vinci and Michelangelo. It has produced some of world's best art, architecture, music, and literature.

2.

3.

Notes

1. Andrea Bocelli, who was blind by age 12, is an internationally celebrated vocalist.

2. Michelangelo, who completed this masterpiece ceiling after four years of standing, insisted he was a sculptor and not a painter.

3. *Pinocchio*, by Carlo Collodi, was originally published as a series in the children's section of a newspaper.

4. Leonardo da Vinci was more than a great artist who created *The Last Supper*. He had one of the best scientific minds of his time.

5. *Aida*, an Italian opera by Giuseppe Verdi, was made into a Broadway musical.

1.

5.

4.

What's for Dinner?

gelato!

Have you ever eaten spaghetti or pizza? Then you've eaten Italian! Italians love food—it is one of the many things they are known for. Below are a few different foods you'll find if you visit Italy!

Minestrone is a popular thick vegetable soup.

Risotto is a rice dish that is mainly eaten in northern Italy.

Cannoli is a popular kind of pastry dessert.

Gelato is Italian ice cream—yummy!

RECIPE

Always ask an adult for help when cooking!

Zuppa Inglese

INGREDIENTS

1 (10 ounce) jar maraschino cherries
1 teaspoon rum flavored extract
1 package instant
   vanilla pudding mix
1 package instant
   chocolate pudding mix

2 (3 ounce) packages ladyfinger cookies
1 pint heavy cream
1 teaspoon white sugar
2 ounces almonds, lightly toasted

mmmmmmmm...this was good!

DIRECTIONS

In a small bowl, drain cherry juice and add rum extract. Set aside. Prepare vanilla and chocolate puddings in separate bowls, according to package directions. Allow to set for 5 minutes.

In a 9x13 inch baking dish, place a layer of cookies on the bottom of the dish. Cut a few of the cookies in order to create a tight fit, if needed.

Sprinkle cookie layer with 1/3 of the cherry juice mixture and spoon vanilla pudding over the cookies, spreading to the edge of the pan. Repeat steps with cookies, cherry juice and chocolate pudding. Make final layer with cookies and remaining juice.

In a medium bowl, whip cream and sugar together until soft peaks form. Top dessert with whipped cream, sprinkle with almonds, and garnish with whole cherries. Refrigerate for 2 hours or more before serving.
Makes 12 servings

Fighting at the Flavian!

What kinds of sports did the ancient Romans like to watch? Gladiator games! And the largest stadium in town was the Flavian Amphitheater. But you probably know it as the Colosseum. Gladiators were professional fighters who battled against each other, wild animals, and slaves. Sometimes these battles were to the death! Most gladiators were slaves, but if they won enough battles, they were sometimes granted their freedom. People would often travel hundreds of miles to Rome to watch the games!

Figure it out!

Figure out the answers to these questions about the gladiators and the Colosseum.

Gladiators who won their freedom were given a wooden sword as a memento.

1. A gladiator needs to win 12 matches to earn his freedom. So far, he's won 3. How many more matches does he need to win?

_____

2. A family needs to travel 630 miles to watch the games at the Flavian Amphitheater. They are halfway there. How many miles have they traveled?

_____

Did you know that the word gladiator comes from the Latin word gladius, meaning "short sword"?

Venice—City of Canals!

Can you imagine a city with no cars—no honking, or traffic jams, or auto accidents? The people of Venice mainly travel by gondola, a long narrow boat, through the city's canals. There are very few cars there!

Venice began as a small fishing community, but quickly grew to be one of the most influential cities in Europe. By the Middle Ages, the people of Venice wanted the world to see that their town was important. The only way for that to happen was for the town to possess the relics of a patron saint. They chose St. Mark, but there was one problem. His bones were in Alexandria, Egypt! Two Venetian merchants stole his bones and smuggled them out in a barrel of pork! To this day, St. Mark is still the patron saint of Venice.

Venice flourished during the Renaissance. It was a city made rich by trade. But by the end of the Renaissance, the city began to decline. The trade route began to shift to the Atlantic, and Venice lost its upper hand in commerce.

Today, Venice is a community of 117 islands and 150 canals. Gondolas are a popular way for tourists to see the city. Venice is also home to the famous Carnevale! Each February, tourists and Venetians alike dress up in elaborate costumes and masks to celebrate. Festivities last for two weeks and end on Ash Wednesday.

Word Fun!

Are these things found in Venice or America? List the words below under the correct heading.

St. Mark's Basilica, jet skis, Renaissance, president, St. Patrick's Cathedral, gondolas, cars, Carnevale, Mardi Gras

> A gondolier is someone who steers a gondola along the Venetian canals. To be a good gondolier, he or she must spend at least two years learning the waterways and tides of the canals!

Venice	America

Italy Did It First!

Mom, Do I Feel Warm?
The thermometer was invented by Galileo Galilei in 1593. His thermometer was a glass bulb containing water. The water moved up or down, depending on the temperature.

All Charged Up!
Count Alessandro Giuseppe Antonio Anastasio Volta, an Italian physicist, invented the chemical battery.

Please Let It Open!
The idea of using a parachute to fall gently to the ground was first written about by Leonardo da Vinci in the late 1400s.

What Goes Down Must Come Up!
Yo-yo's have been used as a toy for over 2,500 years, when the ancient Romans first played with wooden and metal yo-yos.

Let's Play "Chopsticks"!
The modern piano was developed from the harpsichord around 1720, by Bartolomeo Cristofori.

Smooth As Ice!
Frank J. Zamboni (1901-1988) was an Italian-American inventor and mechanic who invented the Zamboni Ice Resurfacing Machine in 1949. It is still used to smooth the ice at most ice rinks around the world.

Can You Hear Me Now?
Guglielmo Marconi made the first radio transmission across the Atlantic Ocean on December 12, 1901.

Do You Feel the Pressure?
The mercury barometer was invented by Evangelista Torricelli, a pupil of Galileo, in 1643. A barometer is a device that measures air pressure.

Word Fun!
This is fun to do with someone else. Ask a friend for words to substitute for the blanks in the story. Their word substitutions will have a humorous effect when the resulting story is then read aloud.

I want to be the first person to _____
(ACTION VERB)

across _____! I've been training for this
(COUNTRY)

since _____. I'm in_____ shape.
(MONTH)   (ADJECTIVE)

My _____ adventure will begin on
(ADJECTIVE)

_____. I won't be hard to miss;
(FAVORITE HOLIDAY)

I'll be the one wearing a _____
(COLOR)

_____ and a pair of matching
(ARTICLE OF CLOTHING)

_____. My faithful friends,
(FOOTWEAR)

_____ and
(FAMOUS ATHLETE)

_____, will be there to cheer for me.
(CARTOON CHARACTER)

I'm bringing my _____ along for good luck.
(NOUN)

I'm confident I'll be the first!

What a Blast!

KABOOM! On August 24, 79 C.E., Mount Vesuvius exploded, shooting volcanic ash and lava over the nearby cities of Pompeii and Herculaneum! People tried to run from the blast, but they never had a chance. Mount Vesuvius continued to erupt for the next 18 hours! Those who might have escaped the eruption were soon killed by a poisonous gas. After three days, both cities were buried under volcanic matter.

As time passed, people abandoned the two cities and their location was forgotten. In the 18th century, archaeologists discovered the lost cities. Much of Pompeii has been uncovered and has given us a snapshot of life at the time. The ash acted as a preservative. Petrified bread was found in the ovens that had been baking that day! Molds of people and animals have been taken, showing the position they were in when they died.

Computer-generated depiction of the eruption of Vesuvius

Mount Vesuvius is still active. Over 3 million people live in its shadow. The last time it erupted was 1944. It is long overdue!

Word Fun!

You are a reporter and are talking to an archaeologist who has just discovered the ancient ruins of Pompeii. What questions would you ask?

Example: How did you discover these ruins?

1. _____?

2. _____?

3. _____?

4. _____?

5. _____?

Vatican City

Vatican City is the smallest country in the world! It is so small that it is actually surrounded by a city—Rome! Vatican City is where the pope lives. The pope is the central authority of the Roman Catholic Church.

Before the arrival of Christianity in Rome, this part of the city had always been sacred. The first church was built on this spot in 326. It is believed that the church lies on the tomb of Saint Peter. As Christianity grew, so did the pope's power. He wasn't just a religious figure but a political one as well. The papacy ruled for more than a thousand years until the mid-19th century. When Italy became a country (rather than individual city-states), most of the Vatican's territory was taken. An agreement was finally reached between the Catholic Church and Italy in 1929. Vatican City officially became an independent state on February 11, 1929.

There are almost 900 people who live in Vatican City. These people are clergy and the Swiss Guard. The Swiss Guard is a volunteer military force that protects the pope. They wear very colorful uniforms of orange and blue! The official language is Latin, but everyone speaks at least one other language.

Vatican City is also home to some of the greatest works of art ever created. St. Peter's Basilica is the largest cathedral in the world. Notre Dame in Paris could easily fit inside of it! The Vatican Museum consists of 54 galleries of art, sculptures, and tapestries, including the glorious Sistine Chapel, Michelangelo's masterpiece.

Vatican City *Photo by David Iliff*

Revealing Answer!

Follow the instructions to reveal the name of the first pope.

1. Cross off the first and last letters.
2. Cross off any letter "O."
3. Cross off the letter that represents the Roman numeral 10.
4. Cross off the first and second "E" from the left.
5. Cross off the fifth letter from the right.
6. Cross off the seventh and last letters of the alphabet.

UGSEOAEXIONXTPOETIZERC

The Italian Renaissance

St. Peter's Basilica's dome was designed by Michelangelo.

Historians consider the Renaissance to be the beginning of modern history. The Renaissance began in 1420 and was inspired by the ancient Greeks and Romans. That would be like people today being inspired to dress, think, and talk as they did in the Victorian era!

"Renaissance" is a French word that literally means rebirth. Scholars became interested in learning about the world around them. Their studies influenced architecture, painting, and sculpture. Many artists were hired by wealthy families or the Catholic Church to produce masterpieces. In many of today's modern Italian cities, you can still see the Renaissance's vast artistic influence.

People today think often think that the Renaissance only affected art. However, all areas of life developed during this time – education, science, philosophy, and politics. Trade routes opened to the Arab world. Merchants prospered as new financial techniques were developed, including bookkeeping and credit. The invention of the printing press helped to spread new ideas and encourage literacy.

The Teenage Mutant Ninja Turtles got their names from famous Renaissance artists: Leonardo (da Vinci), Raphael (Santi), Michelangelo (Buonarroti), and Donatello!

DaVinci's sketch for an ornithopter

Italians flourished during this period and their influence reached all parts of Europe. Eventually, these new ideas and influences would lead some to question the Catholic Church. Still others were encouraged to learn more about the world. This led to the discovery of the New World!

Cross it off!
Starting with the first letter, cross off every other letter to reveal the name of Michelangelo's painted ceiling.

ZSAIDSFTRIFNTERCUHLAIPLEWLX

Just Like Romeo and Juliet

Romeo and Juliet
by Ford Madox Brown

Who were Romeo and Juliet? They were a pair of teenagers who were madly in love with each other. They were characters in a play written by the Englishman William Shakespeare. Romeo Montague and Juliet Capulet met at a masquerade ball and immediately fell in love. After the party, they realized that their fathers were deadly enemies. They were forced to send messages through Juliet's nurse (her nanny). They decided to be together, and Romeo's friend, Friar Laurence, married them. Tragically, however, the two were doomed and ended up dying in each other's arms.

You may wonder what this has to do with Italy. Well, the play takes place in Verona. Today, Verona celebrates the connection every Valentine's Day. Some of the events include a market, a competition for the best love letters, Romeo and Juliet theater, a marathon, and a half-marathon.

Even though the couple did not exist, this has not stopped Verona. A 13th-century building and stables have been converted to represent Juliet's house. Tourists have covered its walls with much scribbling and many love notes stuck on with chewing gum. Juliet's tomb is located in a nearby church. A local volunteer group accepts letters to Juliet. A prize is awarded every Valentine's Day to the best letter. And every September 16, Juliet's birthday is celebrated in the city.

Real or fiction?
Are these people real or fictional? List them under the proper column.

	Real	Fictional
Romeo Montague		
Michelangelo		
Nurse		
Juliet Capulet		
William Shakespeare		
Julius Caesar		
Friar Laurence		
Benito Mussolini		
Lady Capulet		
Leonardo da Vinci		

Italian Fashion

Elegance seems to be in the Italian blood. Italians appreciate beautiful clothing. If you lived in Italy, you would be expected to be well-groomed and have a great sense of style. (A really cool pair of shoes would also help!) No wonder some of the world's best fashion designers are from Italy!

The city of Milan is considered to be the fashion capital of the world. Milan is located in the northwest part of the country and is the home of many famous designers. You may have heard of some of them— Roberto Cavalli, Prada, Ferragamo, Valentino, Versace, and Armani. These designers create unique fashions that are regarded as elegant and glamorous. Many famous Hollywood stars wear Italian fashions and jewelry to dressy events.

Fashion is almost a national passion. If you want to see the latest trends, just visit a restaurant or piazza or watch the people on the streets. Italians always look chic and trendy, but they aren't slaves to fashion. They will always wear something that is flattering to them, but is also durable and comfortable.

Italian fashion is not just about the clothes, but about the attitude. Next time you're in Milan, just watch how the people show off their beautiful fashions! They have an air of confidence and individuality!

Figure it out!

Christina needs your help to get dressed for her tour of Italy! Here are some clothing styles you might see in Italy today. Choose which outfit she'll wear. Color the clothing, and draw a line from the piece of clothing to her or cut the clothing out and dress her up!

Assorted Architecture!

Figure it out!

Use the following clues to figure out the name of this famous building in Rome, Italy.

- Construction of this building lasted from 118 to 126 C.E.
- It was an ancient Roman temple to 12 gods.
- It was saved from ruin by the Catholic Church.
- Enter through the bronze doors to the circular room within.
- The 30-foot oculus in the dome is the only way natural light comes in.
- It is believed that the once-bronze dome was removed and melted down for the canopy in St. Peter's Basilica in 1626.

As They Say in Italy...

Here are a few Italian words you may already know. Why? Because we use them as "English" words all the time!

- **a cappella:** singing without music
- **aria:** a long, accompanied song for one voice
- **ballot:** a sheet of paper used to cast a secret vote
- **bravo:** cry of approval
- **confetti:** small bits of paper made for throwing
- **crescendo:** gradual increase in loudness
- **espresso:** a type of coffee
- **fresco:** a method of painting
- **ghetto:** a quarter of a city in which members of a minority group live
- **graffiti:** unauthorized writing or drawing on a public surface
- **gusto:** enthusiastic and vigorous enjoyment or appreciation
- **influenza:** an illness
- **macaroni:** a type of pasta
- **motto:** a saying
- **pasta:** paste in processed form (as macaroni) or in the form of fresh dough (as ravioli)
- **pizza:** a dish made of flattened bread dough spread with a savory mixture of ingredients and baked
- **prima donna:** first lady
- **regatta:** a boat race
- **solo:** a single performer
- **spaghetti:** a type of pasta
- **stiletto:** a type of shoe
- **vendetta:** revenge

Further Resources

U.S. Embassy in Italy
via Vittorio Veneto, 119/A
00187 Roma, Italy
Phone: (+39) 06.4674.1
Fax: (+39) 06.4674.2356

United Nations
2 United Nations Plaza
New York, NY 10017

Italian Government Tourist Board
630 Fifth Avenue, Suite 1565
New York, NY 10111
Phone: (212) 245-5618
Fax: (212) 586-9249

Interesting Websites

http://www.the-colosseum.net

http://torre.duomo.pisa.it/

http://www.vatican.va

http://www.florenceinitaly.com

Answer Key

Page 7
1. flag 2. symbol 3. motto 4. official
5. population 6. Italy

Page 8
1. B 2. A

Page 9

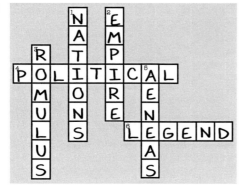

Page 10
6, 1, 3, 5, 2, 4, 7

Page 11
1. B 2. E 3. A 4. C 5. F 6. D

Page 12
Feeding the Christians to the lions – D;
Ides of March – C; Black plague – A;
Niccolo Machiavelli – E; Piazza Novona – B

Page 17
blu	blue
rosso	red
il gatto	cat
l'oliva	olive
il pepe	pepper
sorella	sister
il cane	dog
il bicicletta	bicycle
ciao	hello
grazie	thank you

Page 21
1. 9 matches
2. 315 miles

Page 22
Venice: St. Mark's Basilica, Renaissance, gondolas, Carnevale,
America: jet skis, president, St. Patrick's Cathedral, cars, Mardi Gras

Page 25
Saint Peter

Page 26
Sistine Chapel

Page 27
Real: Michelangelo, William Shakespeare, Julius Caesar, Benito Mussolini, Leonardo da Vinci

Fictional: Romeo Montague, Nurse, Juliet Capulet, Friar Laurence, Lady Capulet

Page 29
Pantheon